CAT FACE

COLORING BOOK

FOR ADULTS

Copyright © 2017 Crystal Coloring Books
All rights reserved.

ISBN-13: 978-1726288187
ISBN-10: 1726288188

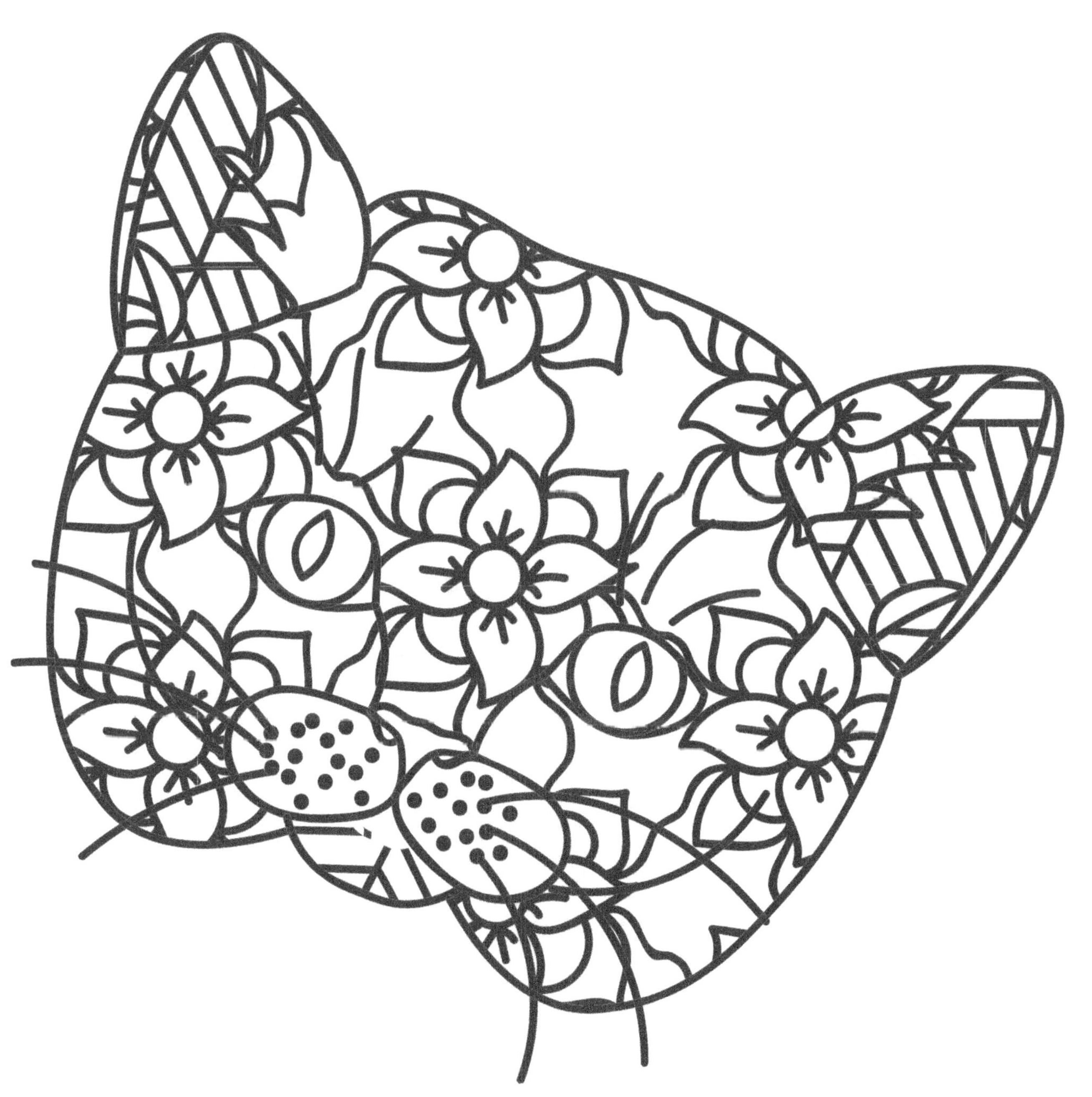

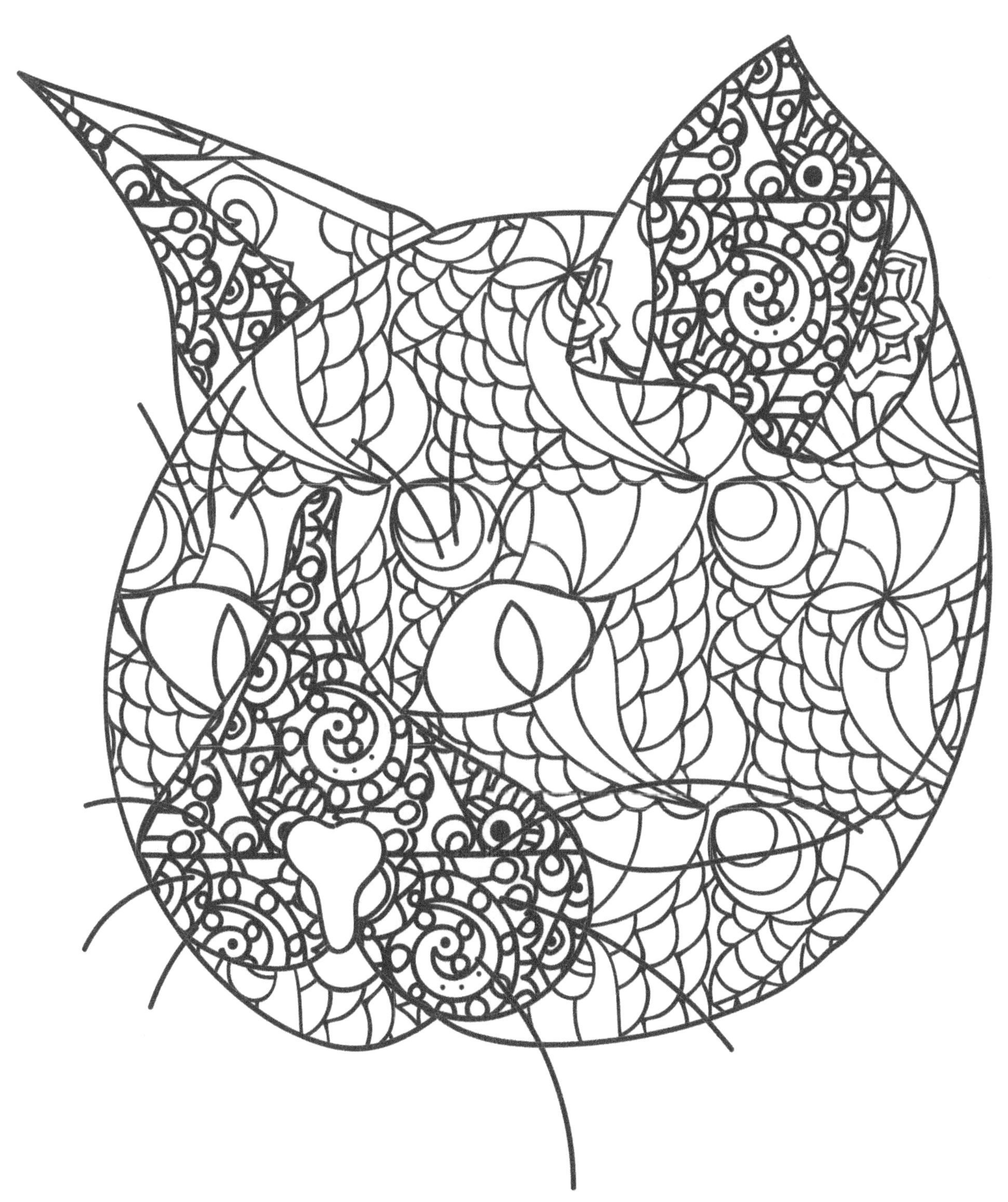

COLOR TEST PAGE

COLOR TEST PAGE

www.ingramcontent.com/pod-product-compliance
Lightning Source LLC
Chambersburg PA
CBHW080238260726
48658CB00008B/3145